Science Fair

Success Guide

Everything You Need to Know to Launch a Winning Science Fair— and Help Students Discover That Science Matters

by Patricia Janes

NEW YORK • TORONTO • LONDON • AUCKLAND • SYDNEY
MEXICO CITY • NEW DELHI • HONG KONG • BUENOS AIRES

Teaching
Resources

Acknowledgments

To my husband, for always being there for me. And to my parents, who
have supported me in everything that I have ever set out to do.

A special thanks to all of the editors of *Science World* and *SuperScience*
who have come before me. You continue to be an inspiration.

Editor: Maria L. Chang
Cover design by Brian LaRossa
Interior design by Jeffrey Dorman

ISBN-13: 978-0-439-89518-7
ISBN-10: 0-439-89518-9
Copyright © 2007 by Scholastic Inc.
All rights reserved.
Printed in the USA.

3 4 5 6 7 8 9 10   40   15 14 13 12 11 10 09 08

Table of Contents

Introduction

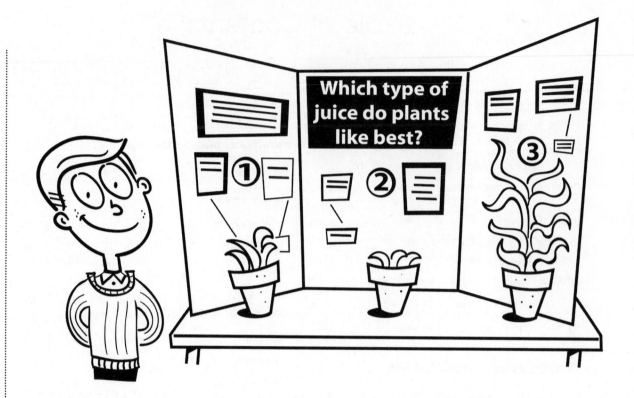

Which type of juice do plants like best?

The fact that you are reading this book likely means one of two things: You have already decided to undertake a science fair with your students, or you are considering it. Either way, you undoubtedly have many questions. What is the value of a science fair? What will it take for me to pull off a successful event? How do I prepare my students for investigative research? Are there any fun alternatives to a traditional science fair? The goal of this book is to answer your questions, and guide you and your students to a meaningful and successful science-sharing experience.

As the executive editor of two Scholastic classroom science magazines for elementary and middle school students, and a former high school science teacher, I have been involved in every aspect of science fairs. I have guided students of all ages—from third to twelfth grade—through the scientific method, walked parents through the steps to helping their child complete a project on time, steered teachers from the concept of a fair to a successful event, and, yes, I have even been charged with choosing the winner from among a sea of eager young scientists. This book wraps all of these experiences into one collection—giving you everything you need to successfully pull off your own science fair.

Science Fair Success Guide contains dozens of reproducible pages that will teach your students to ask testable questions, develop a hypothesis, design and conduct an experiment, collect data, and display their results in a clear and concise manner. With a renewed national emphasis on science education, you will find that these are skills that can be applied to any form of inquiry and investigation—whether the end result is a traditional science fair or a creative alternative. Plus, this book contains teacher checklists, reproducible timetables for parents and students, judging rubrics, reproducible awards, and more.

What is the value of having a science fair?

A science fair is a great way to get kids actively involved in answering a research question—and not just any question, but one that really matches their interests. By following the scientific method to answer that question, students learn to think like a scientist. Even better, a science fair affords kids the opportunity to perform library and Internet research, and get practice in journaling, writing a formal report, and speaking in public.

Plus, science fairs correlate to the National Science Education Standards. In particular, they will help you teach students scientific inquiry.

Are there any proven alternatives to the traditional science fair?

Yes! Schools nationwide have successfully implemented nontraditional science fairs, and this book can easily be adapted to guide you through alternate fairs. If you want to avoid the sense of competition, turn your science fair into a **science expo**, inviting only parents rather than judges.

Or try your hand at a **science carnival**, where students answer a question and develop a carnival game that applies their new knowledge. Invite children from younger grades to enjoy the games—and learn a little science at the same time! Need an example? Which type of balloon rocket moves fastest: a large, long balloon; a medium-size, long balloon; or a large, round balloon? Once students have the answer, set up a booth that challenges carnival visitors to a balloon rocket "race."

You could even work with your gym teacher to hold a **science Olympics**. Every question could relate to sports. Rather than culminate the research with judging, hold a field day that celebrates each sport that the students researched.

The possibilities are endless!

How the Chapters Are Organized

The chapters in this book build upon one another, leading you from the concept of a science fair to the big day. You can use the entire book in sequence, or pick and choose pages according to your needs. Either way, you are sure to experience science fair success!

Chapter 1

Prep Period

Overview

There are five rules to pulling off a successful and enriching science fair.

Rule #1: Organizing a science fair is not rocket science. In fact, with the right planning, it can be downright fun (not that rocket science isn't fun!).

Rule #2: An informed parent can be your best friend.

Rule #3: Involve your school's community, and the overall science-fair experience will be more gratifying—for you and your students.

Rule #4: Picking a science-fair topic is the easy part for most kids. The tough part is coming up with a good question—one that is measurable and testable.

Rule #5: Stay organized. While this rule certainly holds for you, it is geared more toward students. It is important that students document their work—with journals, photos, and data tables—from the moment they begin their projects. It will make writing the report and creating the science-fair display that much easier.

This chapter contains everything from checklists to timetables and invitations. These reproducible pages will help you adhere to the first three rules. (Don't worry: You'll find help with the last two in the following chapters.)

How to Use This Chapter

This chapter contains a combined timetable and checklist designed especially for the teacher so you will know what needs to be done—and by when. Photocopy this checklist so that you can mark it up and still continue to use this book from year to year.

Also included in this chapter are letters for parents to keep them up to speed, from timetables to invitations. An informed parent can fulfill many roles—all of which can help reduce your burden. He or she can help monitor a student's progress, be a cheerleader at home to keep children motivated, volunteer for various duties on the day of the science fair, and generally show support for the fair by attending. Photocopy each of the letters in this chapter, fill in each letter with the appropriate information, and then make enough copies of the completed letters for all your students to take home to their parents.

Lastly, this chapter contains everything you need to involve the community. While the immediate goal of any science fair is, of course, to teach students how to perform investigative research, it is also an invaluable opportunity to showcase what your students are learning in school. Use the reproducible invitations in this chapter to solicit judges from your community.

Checklist for a Successful Science Fair

Below is a checklist that breaks down what you will need to do—and when—to pull off a successful science fair. The checklist is designed with a school-wide fair in mind. Depending on the scope of your science fair, some of the items on this list may or may not be applicable to you.

Teacher Science-Fair Schedule

WEEK	ACTION	DUE DATE	✔
Prior to kick-off	Decide upon the size and scope of your science fair. Will it be school-wide or just for your students? Will it be competitive?		
	Get approval from and coordinate the date with your school principal and/or the director of school activities. Consider times that you might want to avoid, such as the week before holidays or exams.		
	Reserve a location for the science fair, such as the gymnasium, cafeteria, auditorium, or library. Make sure the space is large enough to fit all participating students with their displays, as well as judges.		
	Arrange to borrow tables for the event.		
Week 1	Announce the science fair to students.		
	Discuss the components of a science project with your students: purpose, hypothesis, materials list, and procedure. (See Chapter 2.)		
	Help students identify their interests with the student page: **"What's Your Personality?"** (page 29).		
	Send the parent letter and **"Science Fair Timeline and Checklist"** (pages 10–11) home with students.		
Week 2	Approve students' projects. (For help on choosing a topic and refining questions, see Chapter 3.)		

Teacher Science-Fair Schedule (continued)

WEEK	ACTION	DUE DATE	✔
Week 3	Monitor student progress. Reproducibles in Chapter 4 will help guide students in their work.		
Week 4	Send **"Judge Invitation"** (page 13) to local leaders in the community, asking them to be judges for the science fair. Make sure you invite more than enough judges.		
Week 5	Create a floor plan that shows where each student will set up his or her display.		
Week 6	Send **"Parent Invitation"** (page 12) home with students to invite parents to the science fair.		
Week 7	Using the worksheets from Chapter 5, review with students how to write a formal report.		
	Plan a schedule for school-wide student tours of the science-fair displays. Schedule teacher/parent monitors to be present during student tours.		
Week 8	Send **"Checklist for a Good Display: Do You Have What It Takes?"** (page 54) home to parents so that they can guide students in creating a winning backboard.		
	Ask the school's art classes or art club to design and hang posters announcing the date and location of the science fair.		
Week 9	Prepare students for the interview process with **"Say It!"** (page 55). Have students engage in mock judging interviews to help them anticipate certain questions.		
	Send **"Reminder: Parent Invitation"** (page 12) home with students to remind parents of the science-fair date.		
	Call the judges to remind them of the date, time, and location of the upcoming science fair. Or send them **"Reminder: Judge Invitation"** (page 13).		
Week 10	Have clipboards, pencils, and nametags available for each of the judges on the day of the fair.		

Teacher Science-Fair Schedule (continued)

WEEK	ACTION	DUE DATE	✔
One Day Before the Fair	Have students bring in their displays. If any students forget their displays, remind them to bring them in tomorrow.		
	Encourage students to dress appropriately for the fair!		
Day of the Fair!	Have students set up their displays. Arrange to have custodial help on hand to aid students in the setup and removal of their displays.		
After the Fair	Send thank-you notes to everyone who was involved in the planning, setup, judging, and monitoring of the fair (page 62).		
	Plan a special school-wide announcement of the science-fair winners. Hand out the **"Science Award Winner"** and **"Science Award Participant"** certificates (pages 60–61).		
	Meet with the winning students and their teachers to encourage them to apply to the next level of competition, if one exists.		

From your child's science teacher

Dear Parent:

Your child will be completing a science project this school year, due by _____. A science-fair project challenges a student to solve a question using the scientific method. It is a great way to excite children about science, teach them to think like scientists, develop their organizational skills, and enhance their writing and oral-presentation skills.

I will be giving students handouts in class that explain the process of conducting a science-fair project and guide them on their way. But the bulk of the students' work will be completed at home. I hope that you will offer your child support and encouragement and monitor his or her progress in the coming weeks. At the same time I ask that you keep in mind that the project is your child's responsibility. By limiting your involvement, your child will receive the full educational benefits of the science fair. It should be noted that a successful project does not have to cost a lot of money. Some of the best projects can be completed using materials found around the home!

Attached is a checklist that breaks down the project into manageable pieces, detailing a 10-week plan for completion. I suggest that you use this checklist to help your child plan his or her project and stay on track.

Please contact me if you have any questions. Thank you in advance for supporting your child in such an exciting process of discovery!

Sincerely,

_____ (Science Teacher)

_____ (Phone Number)

_____ (E-mail Address)

Science-Fair Timeline and Checklist

WEEK	ACTION	DUE DATE	✓
Week 1	Make sure you understand what you need to do for your science project. Ask questions if you are unsure about any part of the assignment.		
	Choose a topic: Use the Internet, books, and other library resources. You could also visit museums, zoos, science centers, and so on for project ideas. Keep bibliographic notes on all sources.		
Week 2	With your topic in mind, draft a purpose, hypothesis, materials list, and procedure for your project.		
	Discuss your project with your teacher.		
Week 3	If your teacher approves the project, gather materials and begin your project.		
Week 4	Ask professionals (teachers, doctors, librarians, veterinarians, and so on) for advice and help on how to refine your project and procedure.		
Week 5	Perform your revised experiment and collect data.		
	Keep carefully written records of results in a notebook. Be as specific as you can. Include time of observations, amount, size, and type of materials, and so on.		
	Take photos to document your progress.		
Week 6	Make data tables and graphs to organize your results.		
	Draw conclusions from your results.		
Week 7	Write your project report.		
Week 8	Construct a display. Build a backboard to mount graphs, charts, illustrations, photographs, signs, and summary sheets. Be neat!		
Week 9	Prepare an oral presentation of your work. Practice giving your presentation in front of friends and family members.		
Week 10	Add finishing touches to your project.		
	Present your findings in class or at a science fair.		

From your child's science teacher

Parent Invitation

Dear Parent:

    You are invited to attend your child's science fair! Your child has been working very hard on a science project. Now the time has come for him or her to present the project to members of our community. Your attendance is optional, but I truly look forward to seeing you at this exciting event. Please contact me if you have any questions.

DATE: _____

TIME: _____

PLACE: _____

    We will need volunteers to help students set up their displays for the fair and to ·monitor students on the day of the fair. Are you able to help out? Please check a response below and return this sheet to school with your child by the following date: _____. If you are able to volunteer, I will contact you with more details.

❒ **YES,** I would be happy to volunteer. My phone number is: _____

❒ **NO,** I am unable to volunteer.

Sincerely,

_____ (Science Teacher)

_____ (Phone Number)

_____ (E-mail Address)

From your child's science teacher

Reminder: Parent Invitation

Dear Parent:

    This is a reminder that your child's science fair is quickly approaching and you are invited. I hope to see you on this most-exciting day!

DATE: _____

TIME: _____

PLACE: _____

Sincerely,

_____ (Science Teacher)

_____ (Phone Number)

_____ (E-mail Address)

From the science teacher

Judge Invitation

Dear _____:

    Given that you are a valued leader in the community, I am writing to invite you to be a judge at our school's science fair.

    For several weeks now, my students have been performing scientific research. Soon, they will share their projects and research results with the community. In addition, the projects will be judged and awards will be given to honor the top performers.

    Judges are an important part of our science fair, and I feel that you would make a perfect candidate. I hope that you can take part in our event. Please feel free to contact me if you have any questions.

DATE: _____

TIME: _____

PLACE: _____

RSVP: _____

Sincerely,

_____ (Science Teacher)

_____ (Phone Number)

_____ (E-mail Address)

From the science teacher

Reminder: Judge Invitation

Dear _____:

    I wanted to remind you that the science fair is quickly approaching and that you are slated to be a judge. I look forward to seeing you on this most-exciting day!

DATE: _____

TIME: _____

PLACE: _____

Sincerely,

_____ (Science Teacher)

_____ (Phone Number)

_____ (E-mail Address)

Chapter 2

Get Ready, Get Set

Overview

As soon as you announce the science fair to your students, without a doubt they will be anxious about what the entire process entails. You can be sure that their heads are swirling with questions. Some may be as simple as: *What is a science fair?* or *Will my project be judged?* Others might be more complex: *I forget . . . what are the steps to the scientific method?* This chapter is filled with reproducible pages that will help ease your students' worries.

It starts off with the "Steps to the Scientific Method," which explains to students all of the basic elements of a science-fair project. As helpful as a "cheat sheet" is for students, nothing beats seeing a real science-fair project. So this chapter offers two sample projects—from start to finish—that students can use for reference.

Next follows a list of 200 science-fair questions. Make a copy of all the questions and hand them out to students. These will help get their juices flowing as students start to ponder what they want to study for *their* science-fair project.

How to Use This Chapter

Make copies of the "Steps to the Scientific Method" and hand them out to students on the same day that you announce the fair. Have your students punch holes in this and any other reproducible pages that you give them from this book. Then, have them place each sheet in a binder. By the time you are finished using *Science Fair Success Guide*, your students will have their very own "Science Fair Guidebook."

As a class, read aloud all 200 questions from "200 Science-Project Ideas That Will Wow Judges!" Have students circle the ideas that seem most interesting to them. Then, have them reread the ones that they circled: Do the questions have anything in common? If so, that could lead them to discover an area of science that they find most interesting.

Helpful Tip

Kick off the science fair with some fun. Tell students that they will be creating a "Science Fair Guidebook" over the coming weeks. Then hand out construction paper and colored markers. Encourage students to use their creativity and draw a cover page for their guidebook. Have them use a 3-hole punch and place the cover page inside a ½-inch binder. All of the pages that you hand out in the future can go into this book. And because a binder is sturdy, it should last them through many future science fairs to come!

Steps to the Scientific Method

Name: _____ **Date:** _____

Your teacher has just announced that there's going to be a science fair this year, and that your project needs to follow the scientific method—the step-by-step process that scientists follow when they perform an experiment. Where should you begin? Step One: Don't panic! Step Two: Check out the cheat sheet below. It outlines the scientific method.

1. **Make an observation. Then, propose a research question based on your observation.**

   A good science-fair project question is testable and measurable. For example: *Which brand of bubble gum keeps its flavor longest?* You can test this by chewing different brands of gum and measuring how long the flavor lasts for each brand. The best questions are usually ones that you have a genuine interest in answering.

2. **Identify the variables.**

   A science-fair project involves *variables,* or things that change or could be changed. There are two types of variables: independent and dependent variables. An *independent variable* is one that you change on purpose. For instance, if you were experimenting to find out which brand of gum keeps its flavor longest, you may choose to test three different brands of bubble gum. The *dependent variable,* or the factor that responds to a change in the independent variable, would be the amount of time that the flavor lasts.

   You'll also want to identify your *constants*, or things that will stay unchanged. For instance, you might test only bubble gum that is sugar free. And to make sure that the amount of gum you test is equal each time, you might choose to test only sticks of gum—not gumballs.

3. Research your topic to learn more about it.

Research comes in many forms. You can research a topic by going to the library, performing Internet research, interviewing a scientist, or even speaking with experts at museums, zoos, hospitals, and so on. For our example, you might interview a spokesperson or scientist from a bubble-gum company.

4. Develop a hypothesis, or a possible answer to your question.

Your *hypothesis* should be based on your research. It is important to remember that it is okay if your hypothesis turns out to be wrong. You can learn a lot from any hypothesis—whether it is right or wrong. Your science-fair project will help you test your hypothesis.

5. Design an experiment that will help you answer your research question.

Come up with an experiment *procedure.* This list of steps should be detailed enough so that anyone could read it and repeat the experiment exactly as you performed it.

You will want to run several trials. That means that you'll want to repeat your experiment several times. The more times you repeat the experiment, the more reliable your results will be.

Record your experiment results in a journal. The more notes you take, the easier it will be to type up your report (more on that later). Also, take photos to document your work as you go.

6. Draw conclusions from your results and type up a report that explains your project, results, and conclusions.

The report should be typed and include neat and colorful charts and graphs.

Sample Project One: Stretch Test

Name: _____ Date: _____

Below is an example of a science project from start to finish.
You can use this as your guide as you work on your own project.

Project Topic: How a Person's Flexibility Changes
Throughout a Workout

Project Title: Stretch Test

1. My Question
The question I plan to answer with my
experiment is: Are people able to stretch
farther before or after hanging in a
forward bend?

2. My Purpose
Rewrite your question to complete the
following sentence. The purpose of my
experiment is to: find out when people are
most flexible–at the start or end of a workout.

3. My Variables
My *independent variable*, or the one thing I plan to change, is: the total
length of time spent hanging in a forward bend before giving a stretch test.
   My *dependent variable*, or the change I will measure, is:
the distance that people stretch.
   My *controlled variables*, or the things I will keep the same, are:
people will perform the same stretch test. I will make sure that the room
temperature stays constant throughout the workout because people's
muscles loosen up in warmer temperatures. I will have people perform the
stretch test three days in a row, always at the same time of the day.

4. My Research
Go to the library, perform Internet research, or interview an expert to gather
information about your topic. Keep notes on your findings:
   It is best to do light stretching before a workout and a more thorough
stretching routine after a workout. Stretching your muscles when they're
cold increases your risk of pulled muscles. Source: Mayo Clinic staff,
Stretching: Focus on flexibility, The Mayo Clinic,
http://www.mayoclinic.com/health/stretching/HQ01447

Sample Project One: Stretch Test

(continued)

5. My Hypothesis

A *hypothesis* is a possible answer to a research question. Reread your question in Step 1. Based on my research, my hypothesis is:

The longer a person works out before stretching, the farther the person will be able to stretch.

6. My Procedure

Materials:

ruler

masking tape

clock

pencil

paper

Procedure Steps:

1. Place a ruler on the floor.

2. Use masking tape to tape the ruler to the floor.

3. Ask a person to sit on the floor with his or her legs straight out in front and heels lined up with the ruler's 5-inch mark. Have the person separate his or her heels by 12 inches.

4. Have the person lean forward, arms stretched straight out in front as far as he or she can reach.

5. When he or she can't stretch forward comfortably any more, have the person put his or her fingertips down on the ruler. Record this distance (measure from the 0-inch mark).

6. Have the person stand up and hang in a forward bend for one minute.

7. Repeat Steps 3 through 5.

8. Have the person stand up and hang in a forward bend for another minute.

9. Repeat Steps 3 through 5 once more.

10. Repeat the experiment with the same person for three days in a row. Perform the experiment at the same time each day.

Sample Project One: Stretch Test
(continued)

7. My Data

Independent Variable: Total length of time in forward bend	Dependent Variable: Distance stretched (in inches)			
	Trial 1	**Trial 2**	**Trial 3**	**Average**
0 minute	3 inches	2 inches	4 inches	3 inches
1 minute	4 inches	3 inches	5 inches	4 inches
2 minutes	5 inches	4 inches	6 inches	5 inches

8. Graph of My Data

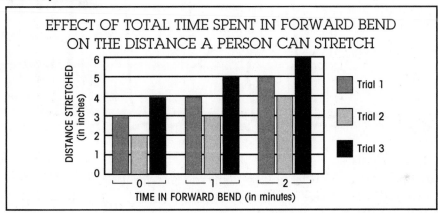

EFFECT OF TOTAL TIME SPENT IN FORWARD BEND ON THE DISTANCE A PERSON CAN STRETCH

9. My Conclusions

Based on my results, I conclude that my hypothesis was correct. The longer a person works out before stretching, the farther the person will be able to stretch. I would like to see how other forms of workout affect the distance a person can stretch. For instance, would doing jumping jacks help a person stretch farther?

10. A Sketch of My Display

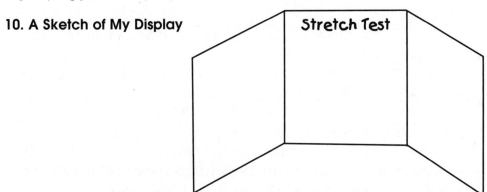

Stretch Test

Sample Project Two: Drip Dry

Name: _____ Date: _____

Below is an example of a science project from start to finish.
You can use this as your guide as you work on your own project.

Project Topic: How Fabric Type Affects
a Cloth's Drying Time

Project Title: Drip Dry

1. My Question
The question I plan to answer with my experiment is:
How does the type of fabric—flannel, cotton, or satin—affect how
long a cloth takes to dry?

2. My Purpose
Rewrite your question to complete the following sentence. The purpose
of my experiment is to:
find out if different materials dry more quickly than others.

3. My Variables
My *independent variable*, or the one thing I plan to change, is:
the cloth's material.
   My *dependent variable*, or the change I will measure, is: the time it
takes for a wet cloth to dry.
   My *controlled variables*, or the things I will keep the same, are:
the cloth's size and shape. I have decided to always use a
standard-size pillowcase and soak each pillowcase in water for the
same amount of time. I will keep the water's temperature constant.
I will place all pillowcases in the same location to dry.

Sample Project Two: Drip Dry
(continued)

4. My Research

Go to the library, perform Internet research, or interview an expert to gather information about your topic. Keep notes on your findings.

I interviewed two experts in fabrics: the owner of my local dry cleaner, who said that satin is a very fast-drying material, and a fashion designer, who said the same thing.

5. My Hypothesis

A *hypothesis* is a possible answer to a research question. Reread your question in Step 1. Based on my research, my hypothesis is:

satin pillowcases will dry faster than flannel or cotton pillowcases. Cotton pillowcases will dry the slowest.

6. My Procedure

Materials:

standard-size satin pillowcase
standard-size cotton pillowcase
standard-size flannel pillowcase
washtub
cold water
bathroom scale
drying rack
bathtub
clock
pencil
paper

Procedure Steps:

1. Weigh each pillowcase and record its dry weight.
2. Fill the washtub completely with cold water.
3. Place all three pillowcases in the water.
4. Leave the pillowcases in the water for 1 hour to soak.
5. While the pillowcases are soaking, set up the drying rack in the bathtub.
6. After allowing the pillowcases to soak for 1 hour, remove them from the water and weigh each one again. Record each pillowcase's wet weight.
7. Hang each pillowcase on a top bar of the drying rack.
8. Close the shower curtain to keep any stray breezes from hitting the towels.
9. Allow the pillowcases to line dry.
10. Weigh each pillowcase every 2 hours.
11. The first pillowcase to reach its dry weight from step 1 is the fastest drying.
12. Continue to let the remaining pillowcases dry. Continue weighing them every 2 hours until all three have reached their dry weight from step 1.

Sample Project Two: Drip Dry
(continued)

7. My Data

Independent Variable: Pillowcase fabric	Dry Weight (in pounds)	Wet Weight (in pounds)	Hour 2 (in pounds)	Hour 4 (in pounds)	Hour 6 (in pounds)	Hour 8 (in pounds)	Hour 10 (in pounds)
Flannel	.4	.8	.8	.7	.6	.5	.4
Cotton	.3	.7	.6	.5	.4	.3	.3
Satin	.2	.6	.5	.3	.2	.2	.2

8. Graph of My Data

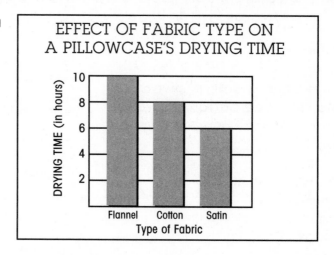

EFFECT OF FABRIC TYPE ON A PILLOWCASE'S DRYING TIME

9. My Conclusions

Based on my results, I conclude that the first half of my hypothesis was correct but the second half was wrong. A satin pillowcase dries faster than cotton or flannel pillowcases. But I also hypothesized that a cotton pillowcase would take the longest to dry. My data shows that the flannel pillowcase took the longest time to dry. If I could do this experiment again, I would use a more sensitive scale. Then I could get more accurate results.

10. My Display

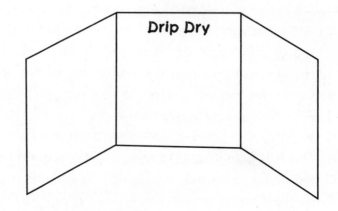

Drip Dry

200 Science-Project Ideas That Will Wow Judges!

Name: _____   Date: _____

Read this list of 200 science-fair project ideas.
Circle all of the ones that sound interesting to you.

1. How does the temperature of a tennis ball affect the height of its bounce?

2. How does the air pressure of a soccer ball affect how far it travels when kicked?

3. Does a metal baseball bat vibrate more than a wooden one?

4. How does the weight of a bowling ball affect how many pins the ball knocks down?

5. Which increases your heart rate more: walking up and down real stairs or using a stair-master?

6. How does yoga affect your flexibility?

7. How does fast dancing affect your heart rate?

8. How does humidity affect the curliness of hair?

9. How does a shampoo's brand affect the strength of hair?

10. How does the type of material affect how long a shirt takes to dry?

11. Which nail polish best resists chipping?

12. How does the fat content of cheese affect its stretchiness?

13. How does the length of time that a soda bottle is open affect its fizziness?

14. How does the temperature of water affect the time it takes to freeze into ice cubes?

15. How will the time spent chewing bubble gum affect its bubbles' maximum size?

16. How will adding different flavors of Kool-Aid® to water affect the water's boiling point?

17. Which brand of popcorn leaves the fewest unpopped kernels?

18. Does the flavor of gelatin affect the amount of time it takes to set?

19. How does playing video games affect hand-eye coordination?

20. What is the effect of toothpaste brand on teeth-cleaning power?

21. What brand of paper towel is most absorbent?

22. What brand of trash bag can withstand the most weight before ripping?

23. How does a light bulb's wattage affect the amount of heat detected above a light?

24. Under what color light do plants grow best?

25. Which brand of mouthwash kills the most bacteria?

26. Which brand of breath mint lasts longest?

27. How does the amount of sugar in homemade ice cream affect how fast it freezes?

28. In a blind taste test, can you tell the difference between nonfat, low-fat, and whole milk?

29. When you pour soda out of a newly opened soda bottle, which produces more fizz: regular or diet soda?

30. How does brand affect ketchup's flow?

31. Given the same amount of water, how does pot size affect the amount of time it takes to boil water?

32. Where is the best place to store home-baked cookies to keep them fresh longest?

33. How does the amount of yeast affect how high bread rises?

34. Which cereal brand stays crunchy in milk the longest?

35. Which brand of chocolate bar melts fastest in the sun?

36. Which type of bread turns moldy first: store-bought or bakery bread?

200 Science-Project Ideas That
Will Wow Judges!

37. How does the type of container affect ice cream's melting time?

38. Which can support more weight: paper or plastic grocery bags?

39. Does the type of animal in a pet-store window affect the number of people who are attracted to the window?

40. Does the color of a terrarium affect a lizard's skin color?

41. Does the brand of kitty litter affect clumping?

42. Does listening to one type of music lower heart rate more than another type?

43. How old does chewed gum have to be before it stops sticking to shoes?

44. Which frozen dessert melts slowest: ice cream, frozen yogurt, or sorbet?

45. How does the tension in a violin's strings affect its pitch?

46. How does the size of a drum affect its pitch?

47. How does a person's age affect his or her flexibility?

48. How does a person's age affect his or her ability to see at night?

49. How does the amount of air in a bicycle's tires affect how long it takes the bike to brake?

50. How does the size of a bicycle's tires affect how far it travels given a specific amount of pedaling?

51. How does hair's curliness affect its strength?

52. How does color affect a person's mood?

53. How does the time of day affect your body's temperature?

54. How does the type of music that a person listens to while exercising affect how hard he or she works out?

55. Does one type of food fill you up faster than another?

56. Which grows faster: fingernails or toenails?

57. Does gender affect lung capacity?

58. If you are right-handed or left-handed, do you also prefer a certain foot?

59. Does the surface of a tennis court affect the height that a tennis ball bounces?

60. Does the time of day affect your flexibility?

61. How does air temperature affect your flexibility?

62. Does a no-name stain remover work just as well as a brand name?

63. Which is a better insulator: wool, cotton, or down feathers?

64. How do various ski waxes affect the amount of friction between the ski and the snow?

65. Does playing Sudoku puzzles improve your performance on other types of puzzles?

66. How does shutter speed affect the color of a photograph?

67. How can you speed up the ripening of tomatoes?

68. What effect does watering have on how fast a plant grows from a seed?

69. How does gravity affect the direction of a plant's growth?

70. Do all plants seek out light?

71. How does the weight of a paper airplane affect its ability to fly?

72. How does a parachute's material affect the speed at which it falls?

73. How does the anticipation of a tickle affect you?

74. How does the weather affect your mood?

75. Which type of soap removes more grease: dish soap, hand soap, or shampoo?

76. Which type of fruit is more acidic: lemons, oranges, or watermelon?

77. What type of ground layers limit erosion most: sand, gravel, or soil?

78. How does the speed of a river's current affect the size of the grains on the riverbed?

79. How does the type of music played in a store affect the number of purchases made by customers?

80. In what type of lighting does a plant grow best?

81. What difference do low-phosphorous fertilizers have on a lake's pollution levels compared with standard fertilizers?

200 Science-Project Ideas That
Will Wow Judges!

82. How does the type of seed in a birdfeeder affect the types of birds that the feeder attracts?

83. What types of flowers attract the highest number of butterflies?

84. Which brand of potato chips has the least grease?

85. How does the material of a bandage affect its ability to stick after getting wet?

86. How does the time of day affect levels of algae in a lake?

87. How does tire pressure affect a car's fuel efficiency?

88. How does the amount of air in a balloon rocket affect how far it flies?

89. How does the type of string used in a "can and string" phone affect the phone's ability to transmit sound?

90. Does one cell-phone carrier get better reception than other carriers?

91. Do "triple roll" toilet paper rolls really last three times as long as regular rolls?

92. Are rooms with carpeted floors noisier or quieter than rooms with wooden floors?

93. How does humidity affect how often a plant needs to be watered?

94. Can people tell the difference between music played on an MP3 player, CD player, tape player, and turntable?

95. How does temperature affect the growth of mold?

96. How does meditation affect your heart rate?

97. Which has a longer life: an LED or an incandescent light bulb?

98. Is the incidence of asthma in a region related to the area's level of air pollution?

99. How does the color of a shirt affect the amount of heat it absorbs?

100. How does the amount of daylight that enters your room affect how late you sleep?

101. How does the type of stuffing in a pillow affect its fluffiness?

102. How does the time of year affect the number of hours of daylight in a 24-hour period?

103. How does the magnification of binoculars affect how far you can see?

104. Do all chocolate candies have the same melting point?

105. Do different types of onions make your eyes tear up more than others?

106. Which is better at cleaning mold and mildew: vinegar or commercial cleaning agents?

107. Does maple syrup's "grade" affect its flow?

108. Do different brands of batteries last longer than others?

109. Which uses more water: a shower or a bath?

110. Which type of cup will keep a hot drink warm longer: paper, plastic, Styrofoam, or glass?

111. Do natural mosquito repellants keep more mosquitoes away than artificial repellants?

112. How do gas stations affect the soil around them?

113. Which cleans teeth more effectively: baking soda or toothpaste?

114. Does the length of a clock's pendulum affect its period?

115. Which holds hair in place for a longer period of time: gel or hairspray?

116. Does listening to music while studying affect your performance on a memory test?

117. Does a person's height affect his or her ability to successfully make a jump shot in basketball?

118. How much trash do you keep out of a landfill by recycling paper and plastics?

119. Which type of photos do people hold on to longer before making prints: digital or film?

120. Do mood rings accurately predict a person's emotions?

121. Is a person's favorite subject in school influenced by gender?

200 Science-Project Ideas That
Will Wow Judges!

122. Does the weight of a baseball bat affect how far the ball goes when it is hit?

123. Does the temperature of a hockey puck affect how far it will travel when struck by the stick?

124. Do girls spend more time talking on the phone with friends than boys?

125. How does the type of food dispensed in school vending machines affect the eating choices that kids make throughout the day?

126. Which type of fertilizer helps plants grow taller?

127. Which has a better chance of survival: grass that was planted as seed or sod?

128. Is there a correlation between gender and the number of push-ups that a person can do?

129. Do best friends have the same favorite color?

130. Who buys from the "sale" rack more often: kids or adults?

131. Are kids more likely to be influenced by ads that feature other kids or by ads that feature adults?

132. Does the amount of time a student spends watching TV affect his or her grades?

133. Does the length of a surfboard affect its stability?

134. Which stays fresher longer: organic or nonorganic fruit?

135. Does a person's age affect whether he or she goes to the Internet, radio, TV, or newspaper for news?

136. Which stains dentures more: coffee, soda, or grape juice?

137. How does the temperature of a pool's water affect the speed at which a swimmer swims?

138. Does the use of flippers help a person swim faster?

139. Do you wake up feeling more alert when you awaken to an alarm clock that buzzes, plays music, or plays nature sounds?

140. Does the size of a dog determine how high or low-pitched its bark is?

141. Does your cat prefer one brand of food over another?

142. Can blindfolded people tell the difference between bottled water and tap water?

143. Is there a relationship between people's age and the amount of time they can hula hoop?

144. Do objects float better in freshwater or in salt water?

145. How does a person's age affect reaction time?

146. How does caffeine affect people's heart rate?

147. Do some materials conduct heat more than others?

148. How does the roughness of sandpaper affect its ability to smooth various surfaces?

149. How does increasing the height of a ramp affect how far a ball rolls down the ramp?

150. How does the strength of a magnetic field vary with the magnet?

151. Can people identify their pet dog by the sound of its bark alone?

152. Do people who exercise regularly have a greater lung capacity?

153. Can people use their sense of hearing alone to tell apart a penny, nickel, dime, and quarter?

154. Do left-handed people prefer the same school subjects as right-handed people?

155. Does the type of liquid in a glass affect the pitch of the note that results when a person rubs the rim of the glass?

156. Does the length of a wind chime affect its pitch?

157. Do people who live in rural areas name constellations correctly more often than people who live in cities?

158. Does weather affect satellite-TV reception?

159. Do girls and boys talk about the same topics as each other when they hang out with their friends?

160. Does the length of a bat affect how far a baseball will travel?

200 Science-Project Ideas That Will Wow Judges!

161. Does your dog prefer water directly from the faucet or tap water that's been refrigerated?

162. How often can people accurately tell if someone is happy, sad, or mad just by looking at the person's eyes?

163. How often can people correctly determine if a person is left-handed or right-handed just by looking at the person's handwriting?

164. What melts ice the fastest: sand, cat litter, or mineral rock salt?

165. Does temperature affect the growth rate of shoots on a potato?

166. Which type of container traps the most heat: a shoebox covered in aluminum foil, plastic wrap, or wax paper?

167. How does the shape of a boat's hull affect its speed?

168. How does water pressure vary with depth?

169. Which best helps prevent soil erosion on a slope: plants, rocks, or mulch?

170. Does one brand of antacid neutralize acids faster than another?

171. Do gym shoes have more bacteria than sandals?

172. Does sunlight fade the paper more in books or in magazines?

173. In which room of the house do plants grow the highest?

174. Which toothbrushes last longest: ones with natural or nylon bristles?

175. Which air freshener lasts longest?

176. Do mildew-resistant shower curtains really keep mildew away longer than regular shower curtains?

177. Does a person's weight vary throughout the day?

178. Do certain bicycle helmets hold up better after an impact than others?

179. Can you skate faster with in-line skates or roller skates?

180. Do thunderstorms happen more often in the afternoon than in the morning?

181. Does bread stay fresher longer when it is kept in the refrigerator or on the counter?

182. Which kind of gum keeps its flavor longer: sugar-free or regular?

183. Which lightens stains better: vinegar or lemon juice?

184. Which type of bread toasts fastest?

185. Do bigger lemons have more seeds than smaller ones?

186. Does squinting improve your vision?

187. Do fans really make you cooler or do they just make you feel like you're cooler?

188. Do taller people take longer strides than shorter people?

189. Can you judge depth as well using just one eye than using two?

190. Does your "handedness" have any relation to which eye is stronger?

191. Does exercise increase or decrease your energy level?

192. How does your sight affect your balance?

193. Which do people prefer: a booth or a table toward the middle of a restaurant?

194. Do plants inside a mall grow faster under artificial light or under a skylight?

195. Does listening to rock music make you eat faster than listening to classical music?

196. Does eye color affect how well a person sees?

197. Does toothpaste with whitener whiten teeth more than regular toothpaste?

198. Does washing your hands reduce the amount of bacteria on them more than not washing?

199. Does using conditioner leave your hair with fewer knots than not using conditioner?

200. Does hair take longer to dry when using a hair drier or when it dries naturally?

Now, reread all of the questions that you circled. Do these questions have anything in common? If so, what?

_____

Look at your answer above. If the questions you circled have anything in common, you probably have a strong interest in that topic. You might want to think about doing a science-fair project on that topic.

Chapter 3

What to Do?

Overview

Students often find that two of the most challenging aspects of performing a science-fair project are choosing a topic and deciding if their question is a good one. This chapter begins with a personality test that will help students learn more about their interests. Combined with the list of 200 science-fair questions from Chapter 2, most students will now be at a point where they feel comfortable choosing a topic. The chapter then moves on to teaching students what makes a good science-fair question—one that is both testable and measurable.

The remainder of the chapter teaches students about each of the main components of a science-fair project: how to perform research prior to experimenting, how to write a procedure, how to design an experiment, and how to keep organized tables. It also provides reproducible worksheets that enable students to practice reading bar graphs, line graphs, and pie charts.

How to Use This Chapter

The reproducible "What Makes a Good Question?" will likely prove to be the most difficult one in this book for your students to complete. But it is also one of the most important. Take time to review students' answers and work together as a class to examine responses and decide which ones make for the best project questions and why. If your class is still struggling with what makes a good question, group students into teams and challenge them to come up with a list of "bad questions" that the opposing team has to rewrite as "good questions."

The remaining pages are good science-fair discussion starters. For example, have students read aloud their responses from "How Did You Do That?"—which challenges students to write a detailed procedure describing the steps to brushing your teeth. As a class, evaluate if any steps are vague, or if any steps are missing. Together, write on the board the ideal procedure. Encourage students to add each reproducible worksheet from this chapter into their binder that they created at the start of Chapter 2 for future reference.

Helpful Tip

Before handing out "How Did You Do That?" to students, use the following tried-and-true activity with your class. It will reinforce the importance of writing a detailed procedure: Get a bag of bread, a jar of jelly, a jar of peanut butter, and a plastic knife or spoon. Ask students to write on a piece of paper a detailed list of the steps involved in making a peanut-butter-and-jelly sandwich. Then, have them tell you their steps. Follow their instructions exactly. So if someone says, "Take out a piece of bread," take a piece of bread out into the hall. If they ask why you did that, prompt them to realize that their step was a bit vague. A better step would have been "Take a piece of bread out of the bag."

What's Your Personality?

Name: _____ **Date:** _____

Take the multiple-choice quiz below to learn more about your personality.
Then flip the page upside down to score yourself. Use that information to guide you
to a science-fair project that is just right for you!

1. It's Saturday night and you're looking for something fun to do. You
   a. call up your best friend to chat for a while.
   b. strap on your in-line skates and go for a spin.
   c. pull out your pottery wheel and make a bowl.
   d. flip on your Gameboy® and try to beat your best score.

2. Your mom takes you to the mall. You make a beeline for
   a. the food court—that's where your friends hang out.
   b. the sports store—you need a new soccer ball.
   c. the craft store—you've been wanting to learn to knit.
   d. the electronics store—you want to buy the newest gadget.

**3. When someone asks you what you want to be when you grow up,
   you're most likely to answer**
   a. teacher.
   b. pro athlete.
   c. artist.
   d. video-game designer.

**4. As part of a school assignment, you have to build something.
   You decide to build**
   a. a tree house where your secret club can meet.
   b. a pitching machine so you can practice your swing.
   c. an easel to hold your canvas as you paint.
   d. a transistor radio using the do-it-yourself kit that you got for your birthday.

5. If there were one thing you couldn't live without, it would be
   a. your best friend.
   b. your baseball that's signed by baseball legend Babe Ruth.
   c. your sketch pad.
   d. your MP3 player.

If you answered mostly:

A's, you're a social butterfly. Try to think of a science experiment that answers a question about people's behavior. For example: Do girls and boys talk about the same topics when they hang out with their friends?

B's, you're a sports fanatic! You might enjoy an experiment that deals with athletics. For instance: Does the length of a bat affect how far a baseball will travel?

C's, you're artistic. You might enjoy a project that deals with the arts, like painting, writing, or acting. For example: Do watercolor paints tend to run more on certain types of surfaces than on others?

D's, you're into the latest gadgets. Consider doing a project that involves technology. Here's an idea: How does the weather affect satellite-TV reception?

What Makes a Good Question?

Name: _____ **Date:** _____

The key to a good science-fair project is coming up with a good question. But what makes a good question? It should be measurable and testable. The questions below are <u>not</u> good science-fair questions. Rewrite each question to make it measurable and testable. See the examples below. (Hint: There is more than one right answer. There are many ways to turn these questions into good ones!)

Example 1:

Bad Question: How is one brand of battery different from another?

Good Question: Which lasts longer: a brand-name battery or a store-brand battery?

Example 2:

Bad Question: Which brand of popcorn is best?

Good Question: Which brand of microwave popcorn leaves the fewest unpopped kernels?

1. **Bad Question:**   Is one brand of cereal better than another?

   _____

2. **Bad Question:**   Is it bad to watch TV while studying?

   _____

3. **Bad Question:**   Does staying up late make you tired?

   _____

4. **Bad Question:**   Are you flexible?

   _____

5. **Bad Question:**   How well does a paper airplane fly?

   _____

6. **Bad Question:**   Does practice really make perfect?

   _____

7. **Bad Question:**   How can a baseball player hit the ball farther?

   _____

8. **Bad Question:**   Can a paper towel absorb milk?

   _____

9. **Bad Question:**   How can you keep hot chocolate warm?

   _____

10. **Bad Question:**   Is skating good exercise?

    _____

Give Credit Where It's Due

Name: _____ **Date:** _____

Before starting your science experiment, you'll need to do some research to learn more about your project idea. For this you can go to the library, search the Internet, or even interview an expert. No matter where you go to gather information, you'll need to keep track of your sources and take good notes. Below are some rules to giving credit to your sources.

If you get information from:

1. **a Web site,** write down the author or editor of the source (if given), title of the document or posting, name of the institution sponsoring the Web site, date when you visited the Web site, and the URL. (Note: If the URL is very long, list the URL of the Web site's search page.)
   For example: *Amusement Park Physics*. Annenberg Media.
   18 December 2006.
   <http://www.learner.org/exhibits/parkphysics/index.html>

2. **a CD-ROM encyclopedia,** write down the subject, the name of the program, the name of the supplier, and the year of publication.
   For example: "Plant Distribution." *Encarta*. Microsoft, 1999.

3. **a book,** write down the author's name, book title, place of publication, copyright date, pages that you read.
   For example: Berger, Melvin and Gilda. *Why Don't Haircuts Hurt?* New York: Scholastic, 1998: 4–6

4. **a magazine,** write down the author's name, title of the article, title of the magazine, issue date, the volume and issue number, and page numbers.
   For example: Bryner, Jeanna. "Catch the Wave." *SuperScience*. May 2006, Vol.17, Iss.8: 6–9

5. **a newspaper,** write down the author's name, title of the article, title of the newspaper, edition date, and page numbers.
   For example: Hellmich, Nanci. "Study Suggests Eating Slowly Translates to Eating Less." *USA Today*, 11/16/2006, D.5

6. **an encyclopedia,** author (if given), the subject, name of encyclopedia, date of publication.
   For example: Adams, Clark E. "Hamster." *The World Book Encyclopedia*, 2001.

7. **an interview,** name of the person interviewed, kind of interview (for example, in person, phone interview, e-mail interview), and the date.
   For example: Stephen Hawking, e-mail interview, 11/3/06

How Did You Do That?

Name: _____ **Date:** _____

A well-written procedure is so detailed that anyone who reads your steps should be able to follow them and perform the experiment exactly the way you did. Below, write a detailed procedure for how to brush your teeth. Then compare what you wrote with what your classmates wrote. Do you notice any differences among the procedures?

_____

_____

_____

_____

_____

_____

_____

_____

_____

_____

_____

_____

_____

_____

Perfecting Your Procedure

Name: _____ **Date:** _____

Suppose you want to conduct an experiment to answer the research question: *What brand of paper towel is most absorbent?* The following is a very basic description of the steps you would take to answer your question. Think about how you would conduct the experiment and rewrite the procedure on a separate sheet of paper. Make it very detailed so that someone else could repeat your experiment exactly the way you did it.

Procedure:

1. Purchase different brands of paper towels.

2. Let them soak in a liquid.

3. Squeeze all of the absorbed liquid out.

4. Measure how much liquid each brand absorbed.

5. Compare your results.

Stay Cool

Name: _____ **Date:** _____

Suppose your friend conducted an experiment to find out what type of container keeps ice cream from melting longest. Below is your friend's data table. Look at the data to answer the questions that follow.

THE EFFECT OF CONTAINER TYPE ON ICE CREAM'S MELTING TIME

Type of Container	Melting Time (in minutes)			
	Trial 1	Trial 2	Trial 3	Average
Paper	60	58	62	60
Plastic	47	54	52	51
Styrofoam	77	75	73	75

Questions:

1. How many trials for each type of cup did your friend conduct?

_____

2. What was your friend's *independent variable*, or the detail that was changed on purpose?

_____

3. What was your friend's *dependent variable*, or the variable that changed in response to a change in the independent variable?

_____

4. On average, in which cup did the ice cream melt fastest?

_____

5. What can you conclude from your friend's results?

_____

_____

A-maze-ing Fish

Name: _____ **Date:** _____

Suppose you have a pet fish that happens to be very smart. For this year's science fair, you've decided to answer the question: *Does the number of twists and turns in a maze affect the time it takes for my fish to swim through the maze?* Using materials from around the house, you rig up a maze in the fish tank and time your fish as it swims through the maze. You time your fish against various mazes, each with a different number of twists and turns. Below is a bar graph of your results. Use the data to answer the questions that follow.

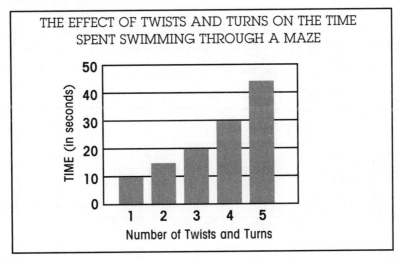

Questions:

1. What was your *independent variable*, or the detail that you changed on purpose?

   _____

2. What was your *dependent variable*, or the variable that changed in response to a change in the independent variable?

   _____

3. With what number of twists and turns could your fish navigate fastest?

   _____

4. Approximately how many more seconds did it take your fish to swim through a maze with five twists and turns compared to a maze with just two?

   _____

5. Based on the data shown on the bar graph, what can you conclude?

   _____

   _____

Kitten Craze

Name: _____ **Date:** _____

Suppose you just got a new kitten. For your science-fair project, you've decided to track your kitten's weight to see if it gains weight more quickly when it is younger than it does when it is older. Under your parents' supervision, you give your kitten the same amount of food and water each day. Every Saturday morning for eight weeks, you weigh your kitten. Below is a line graph of your results. Use the graph to answer the questions that follow.

How a Kitten's Age Affects Its Weight Gain

Weight (in ounces)

30
25
20
15
10
5
0

1 2 3 4 5 6 7 8

Week

Questions:

1. What was your *independent variable*, or the detail that you changed on purpose?

_____

2. What was your *dependent variable*, or the variable that changed in response to a change in the independent variable?

_____

3. What did you keep *constant* throughout your experiment?

_____

4. Between which two weeks did your kitten gain the most weight?

_____

5. Based on the data shown on the line graph, what conclusions can you make?

_____

_____

Sports Score

Name: _____ **Date:** _____

This year, even the teachers are getting involved in the school science fair! Your gym teacher is performing an experiment on—what else—sports! As part of his experiment, he surveyed 100 sixth graders to learn what their favorite sport in gym class is. At the science fair, your gym teacher displays the pie chart below. Look at the pie chart, and then answer the questions that follow.

TYPE OF SPORT IN GYM CLASS
THAT SIXTH GRADERS PREFER

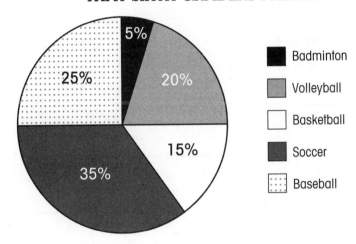

■ Badminton

▨ Volleyball

□ Basketball

■ Soccer

▦ Baseball

Questions:

1. Among sixth graders surveyed by your gym teacher, which sport is the least favorite?

    _____

2. How many students prefer basketball? _____

3. How many more students prefer baseball over volleyball? _____

4. If your gym teacher had to remove one sport from gym class, which one should he remove? Why?

    _____

5. What conclusions can you reach from your gym teacher's science-fair display?

    _____

Chocolate Lover's Experiment

Name: _____ **Date:** _____

There are so many tasty varieties of chocolate: plain, candy-coated, cups with peanut-butter centers. But which one will last longest under the heat of the sun? Design an experiment to find out. Then answer the questions below.

1. What is your *independent variable*, or the detail you would change on purpose?

    _____

2. What is your *dependent variable*, or the variable you would measure?

    _____

3. State your *research question* for this experiment.

    _____

4. State your *hypothesis*.

    _____

5. List the *materials* you'll need for this experiment.

    _____

6. On a separate sheet of paper, write a detailed *procedure* to test your hypothesis. Remember: Other people who read your paper should be able to follow your instructions exactly.

7. Identify your *control*.

    _____

8. What variables should you hold *constant*?

    _____

9. On a separate sheet of paper, design a *data table* for recording your results.

10. What kind of *graph* or *chart* would you use to present your data? Draw your graph or chart on a sheet of graph paper.

Chapter 4

Project Time!

Overview

The reproducible worksheets in previous chapters introduced students to all aspects of a science-fair project and gave them practice with individual components like identifying variables, writing a procedure, and reading graphs. This chapter goes a step further: It contains a formatted journal that students can fill in as they begin researching and experimenting. The journal will help guide students along the way, ensuring that they remember to complete each step of a science-fair project. It also contains a how-to guide for making data tables, bar graphs, line graphs, and pie charts. These pages go into the nitty-gritty details, such as which variable—independent or dependent—should be placed along a graph's x-axis.

How to Use This Chapter

Photocopy each reproducible worksheet in this chapter for students. Encourage them to use the journal pages as a guide. If they need additional room for notes, procedure steps, and so on, have them use a notebook or add loose-leaf paper to their binders. Also, have them refer to the various "how-to" guides for making tables, charts, and graphs as they compile their results independently at home. And while these are student pages, they'll also serve as a cram course for parents as they help their children prepare their written reports and displays.

Helpful Tip

Have students place the pages from this chapter into their binders. That way, you can check the journal entries periodically to monitor students' progress.

My Science Journal
(Worksheet 1)

Name: _____ **Date:** _____

Use the following worksheets to stay organized.

Project Topic:

_____

Project Title:

_____

1. My Question
The question I plan to answer with my experiment is: _____

_____

2. My Purpose
Rewrite your question to complete the following sentence. The purpose of my experiment is to:

_____

3. My Variables
My *independent variable*, or the one thing I plan to change, is:

_____

My *dependent variable*, or the change I will measure, is:

_____

My *controlled variables*, or the things I will keep the same, are:

_____

4. My Research
Go to the library, perform Internet research, or interview an expert to gather information about your topic. Keep notes on your findings. List your resources on the back of this page.

5. My Hypothesis
A *hypothesis* is a possible answer to a research question. Reread your question in Step 1. Based on my research, my hypothesis is:

_____

My hypothesis is based on these facts that I gathered during my research:

_____

My Science Journal

(Worksheet 2)

Name: _____ **Date:** _____

6. My Procedure

Materials:

_____

_____

_____

_____

Procedure Steps:

_____

_____

_____

_____

_____

_____

_____

_____

_____

_____

_____

_____

_____

My Science Journal

(Worksheet 3)

Name: _____ **Date:** _____

7. My Data

(You may not need all of the rows in this data table. If you need more rows, ask your teacher for a second copy of this worksheet. If this data table doesn't seem right for your project, ask your teacher for help.)

Independent Variable (Describe the thing that you will change in your experiment)	Dependent Variable			
	Trial 1	Trial 2	Trial 3	Average (Add the three numbers from your trials. Then divide by three.)

My Science Journal

(Worksheet 4)

Name: _____ **Date:** _____

8. **Graph of My Data** (If you have more than one graph, ask your teacher for a second copy of this worksheet.)

TITLE: _____

label this axis

label this axis

9. **My Conclusions** (What did you learn from your experiment results? Does your conclusion support your hypothesis? If not, based on your results, what would be your new hypothesis?)

_____

_____

_____

_____

_____

How to Make a Data Table

Name: _____ Date: _____

Data tables keep your experiment results organized. Here are the steps to making a data table:

1. On a plain sheet of paper, use a ruler to draw a data table like the one shown below.

2. Give your table a title that describes your variables ("The Effect of Different Types of Movies on Heart Rate").

3. Label the column on the left as the independent variable (Type of Movie). Underneath, list each type of movie you used for the independent variable (Drama, Comedy, Horror).

4. Label the columns to the right as the dependent variable (Heart Rate (beats per minute)). Draw boxes under these columns in which you can record the result of each trial for each independent variable.

5. Include a column to record the average result for each independent variable. To calculate the average result for each independent variable, just add the results of all trials for a particular independent variable. Then divide the total by the number of trials. Repeat this for the remaining independent variables.

The Effect of Different Types of Movies on Heart Rate

Type of Movie	Heart Rate (beats per minute)			
	Trial 1	Trial 2	Trial 3	Average
Drama	89	90	91	90
Comedy	92	92	95	93
Horror	104	99	100	101

How to Make a Bar Graph

Name: _____ **Date:** _____

A bar graph is an easy way to see how independent variables compare with each other. Here are the steps to making a bar graph:

1. On graph paper, draw a set of axes. The horizontal line is your x-axis. The vertical line is your y-axis.

2. Give your bar graph a title that describes your variables ("The Average Effect of Different Types of Movies on Heart Rate").

3. Label the horizontal (x) axis with your independent variable (Type of Movie), including a label of each type of movie (Drama, Comedy, Horror).

4. Label the vertical (y) axis with your dependent variable (Heart Rate (beats per minute)) and a scale from 0 to at least the highest number in your dependent variable results.

5. For each independent variable, draw a solid bar to the height of the corresponding value of the dependent variable. For example, the average heart rate while watching a drama is 90 beats per minute. Draw a bar above the "Drama" label on the x-axis to the 90-beats-per-minute mark on the y-axis.

The Average Effect of Different Types of Movies on Heart Rate

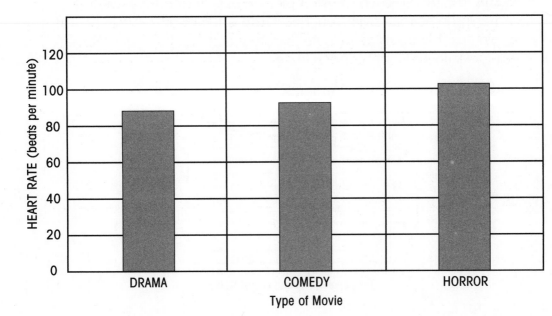

How to Make a Line Graph

Name: _____ **Date:** _____

Choose to make a line graph when you want to see how changes to the independent variable over time affect the dependent variable. Here are the steps to making a line graph:

1. On graph paper, draw a set of axes. The horizontal line is your x-axis. The vertical line is your y-axis.

2. Give your line graph a title that describes your variables ("The Effect of Time Spent Watching Horror Movies on Heart Rate").

3. Label the horizontal x-axis with your independent variable (Time Spent Watching Horror Movies (in minutes)) and a scale with the values of the independent variable (0, 2, 4, etc.).

4. Label the vertical y-axis with your dependent variable (Heart Rate (beats per minute)). Use a scale from 0 to at least the highest number in your dependent variable results.

5. Plot a point on the graph for each piece of data. For example, suppose your heart rate after watching 2 minutes of a horror movie is 95 beats per minute. To locate the point on your graph, draw an imaginary vertical line from the 2-minute mark on the x-axis. Then, draw an imaginary horizontal line from the 95-beats-per-minute mark on the y-axis. Plot the point where the imaginary lines intersect.

6. Once you have plotted the points for all of your data, connect the points to form a line. So for example, suppose that after 4 minutes of watching a horror movie, your heart rate is 100 beats per minute; after 6 minutes, 105 beats per minute. Before watching the horror movie (0 minutes), it was 85 beats per minute.

The Effect of Time Spent Watching Horror Movies on Heart Rate

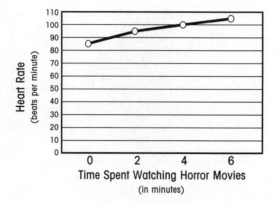

How to Make a Pie Chart

Name: _____ **Date:** _____

Use a pie chart to show numbers expressed as a percentage of a whole. A pie chart is a circle divided into wedges the shape of pizza slices. The circle represents 100 percent. The wedges represent data that are percentages of a whole. Suppose you took a poll at a movie theater asking 100 moviegoers which type of movie they prefer: comedy, drama, or horror. The number of moviegoers you surveyed represents 100 percent. And each type of movie, as selected by the percentage of moviegoers, represents a different wedge of the pie chart. Here are the steps to making a pie chart:

1. Draw a circle with a compass.

2. Give your pie chart a title that describes your variables ("Type of Movie That Moviegoers Prefer").

3. Mark the center with a point; this is where each pie wedge will start.

4. Measure a wedge for each independent variable (Drama, Comedy, or Horror). First, convert your data from percentages to angle degrees. For example, if 25% of moviegoers prefer dramas, the pie wedge for dramas would be 25% of the 360-degree circle, or 90 degrees. Then, position a protractor at the center point of the circle. Mark 0-degree and 90-degree angles with points on the edge of the circle. Draw a line from these points to the center of the circle.

5. Label the wedge (include its percentage).

6. Measure your next wedge from the edge of the first. When you are finished, the entire circle should be filled in and add up to 360°. The percentages should add up to 100%.

Type of Movie That Moviegoers Prefer

20% Horror
25% Drama
55% Comedy

Chapter 5

Show Off!

Overview

Students may be finished conducting their experiments, but they aren't finished with their science-fair projects! Now that the results are in, it's time for students to analyze the data and draw conclusions. Only then will they know if their hypotheses were correct or incorrect.

This chapter will guide students through the process of writing a formal science report. It describes each component of a written report: title page, table of contents, summary, statement of purpose, statement of hypothesis, experiment section, data section, conclusions section, and bibliography.

Several pages of this chapter are also devoted to creating a display. These worksheets cover everything from the size regulations of backboards to how best to organize the display. "Plan Your Display" encourages students to sketch their display ideas on paper before committing them with glue to the backboard.

The chapter concludes with reproducible worksheets that you've probably been looking forward to since day one: pages that prepare students for the day of the science fair. These include interview tips for when the judges stop by a student's booth, science fair dos and don'ts, and a science-fair survival kit.

How to Use This Chapter

If a student has never taken part in a science fair, he or she may have no concept of what a display looks like. Reproduce the student pages in this chapter. As a class, discuss the differences between a written report and a display. Ask students what the strengths and weaknesses are for each method of communicating project results. For example, a report is a good way to explain the project in depth whereas a display is a good way to show off a project's highlights.

Encourage students to role-play as a way to practice for the interview questions that judges might ask them on the day of the science fair. Recommend to students that they practice their interview skills with parents, siblings, or friends at home, too.

Hand out the worksheet of "Science Fair Dos and Don'ts" a few days prior to the fair. The day before the fair, review proper science-fair behavior with students.

Helpful Tip

Remember Rule #2 from Chapter 1: "An informed parent can be your best friend"? Send "Checklist for a Good Display: Do You Have What It Takes?" and "Checklist: What to Bring on the Day of the Science Fair" home with students. By involving parents in the science-fair project display and the science-fair survival kit, your chances of having a class full of prepared students on the day of the fair multiply.

Write It!

Name: _____ **Date:** _____

Congratulations! You have completed all of the hard work! Now it is time to show off your efforts by writing a report that describes your entire project experience. A project report documents your work from start to finish. But more importantly, it allows the reader to know exactly what your project was all about: what your purpose and hypothesis were, how you performed your experiment, what data you gathered, what your conclusions were, and whether or not your conclusions support your hypothesis. Think of your written report as your spokesperson while you are away from your project, for example, during pre-judging that might occur at the science fair.

If you kept a good journal along the way, writing your project report should be a cinch! For the most part, your report will be a neater, more organized version of your journal. It will also include tables, graphs, charts, and any photos you may have taken of your project. Unless your teacher says otherwise, your report should be typed double-spaced.

Your science-project report should contain the following:

1. **A title page.** This page is your report's cover. It should contain a snappy title that reflects the subject matter of your project. This text should be centered in the middle of the page.

2. **A table of contents.** The table of contents lists every major section of your report. It should include the page on which each of the major sections can be found.

Write It!
(continued)

Name: _____ **Date:** _____

3. **A summary.** The summary is a brief overview of your project. It states your project title, the purpose of your experiment, your hypothesis, a brief description of your procedure, and your conclusions. Your summary should be between 250 and 300 words long.

4. **A statement of purpose.** The purpose should clearly explain the goal of your project.

5. **A statement of your hypothesis.** Your hypothesis should be a possible answer to your research question based on the background research that you performed.

6. **An experiment section.** The experiment section of your report should clearly outline your purpose, your variables and controls, your full materials list, your procedure, and your data-collection methods. Remember: Your procedure is a detailed list of the steps that you performed throughout your experiment. A well-written procedure is so detailed that anyone who reads your steps should be able to follow them and perform the experiment exactly as you did it.

7. **A data section.** The data section of your report should show all of the data that you gathered during your experiment in an organized way. All of your data should appear in colorful, neatly labeled tables, graphs, and charts.

8. **A conclusions section.** The conclusions section of your report summarizes what you discovered based on your experiment results. It should restate your hypothesis and tell whether or not your data supports it. This is also a good place to write any questions that arose from your experimentation and any project extensions that you would like to do in the future. You should keep your conclusion to one page.

9. **A bibliography.** A bibliography is a complete list of sources that you used during your research.

10. **Appendices** (optional). An appendix can include anything else that you feel would help to explain your project. It could include diagrams, articles, interviews, additional tables, graphs, charts, or photos.

10 Tips to Creating a Winning Display

Name: _____ **Date:** _____

Your project display is the first thing that people will see when they stop by your booth at the science fair—so you'll want it to look fabulous!

What is a display? A science-fair display is made up of a sturdy backboard that shows off the key points of your project. Your display should include the following: project title, your question, hypothesis, experiment (including materials and procedure), data (including tables, graphs, charts, and photos if you have some), results, conclusions, and future experiment plans. Your display should also include your science-project report and any other items that will help people understand your project, like models or equipment that you used during your experiment.

It is important that your display be neat, colorful, and organized. Below are some tips to designing an award-winning display.

1. Your backboard should be an upright board that sits on top of a table and is able to support itself. It is usually three-sided, but it does not have to be.

2. The backboard should be no larger than 108 inches (274 cm) high, including the exhibit table, 30 inches (76 cm) deep, and 48 inches (122 cm) wide.

3. You can either buy a pre-made backboard or build your own from heavy cardboard or pieces of wood, attached by hinges. Steer clear of thin poster board or cardboard because they bend too easily. A company called Showboard sells pre-made backboards (www.showboard.com or 1-800-323-9189).

4. Use computer graphics or self-stick letters to create headings for each part of your display. Make sure your lettering is easy to read.

10 Tips to Creating a Winning Display

(continued)

Name: _____ **Date:** _____

5. Type the following parts of your display. Use spell check before you print out the pages. Also, remember that you have limited space on your backboard, so plan ahead.

   • **Project title:** Your project title should be large enough to be read from a distance of roughly 3 feet (1 meter). Use larger letters for your title than for anything else on your board. This will help it to stand out.

   • **Your question**

   • **Your hypothesis**

   • **Experiment** (including materials and procedure): Summarize your experiment so that it fits on one or two sheets of paper.

   • **Data** (including tables, graphs, charts, and possibly even photos): If possible, use a color printer to create colorful graphs and tables.

   • **Results:** Summarize your results so that they fit on one sheet of paper.

   • **Conclusions:** Your conclusions should be a summary of what you learned. You should try to do this in a paragraph or two. Also, say whether or not your hypothesis is correct.

   • **Future experiment plans:** As you experimented, you probably thought up new questions, or even how you might do the experiment differently if you were to do it again. Share those ideas in this section.

6. Use colors on your display, but don't get too flashy or the colors could be distracting.

7. Before you stick anything to your backboard, lay the letters and pages onto the board. Space things out evenly and neatly. Rearrange things until it looks just right!

8. Use rubber cement or double-sided tape to post your papers. Avoid using white school glue because it can cause paper to wrinkle.

9. Don't forget to gather any models or other props that you'll want to display on the day of the science fair.

10. Don't forget that your project report and project summary are part of your display! When you set up your display at the science fair, remember to place them on the table in front of your backboard.

Plan Your Display

Name: _____ **Date:** _____

Use a pencil and this blank backboard panel to sketch out how you plan to arrange your display. Erase and sketch again until you are happy with the way your display looks!

Keep in mind that your display should include all of the following: project title, your question, hypothesis, experiment (including materials and procedure), data (including tables, graphs, charts, and photos if you have some), results, conclusions, and future experiment plans. Usually, your project title should be centered at the top of the middle panel.

	Project Title	

Checklist for a Good Display: Do You Have What It Takes?

Name: _____ Date: _____

Does your display have what it takes to wow the judges? Below is a checklist of what judges are looking for when they stop by to check out your display. Before you attach anything to your backboard, make sure you have checked everything off this list!

❏ Does your backboard meet the size requirements?

(no larger than 108 inches (274 cm) high, including the exhibit table,

30 inches (76 cm) deep, and 48 inches (122 cm) wide)

❏ Can your backboard stand up all on its own?

❏ Does your display include all of the following?

____ Project title

____ Your question

____ Hypothesis

____ Experiment (including materials and procedure)

____ Data (including tables, graphs, charts, and possibly even photos)

____ Results

____ Conclusions

____ Future experiment plans

❏ Is your display arranged in a way that is easy to follow and understand?

❏ Are your project title and other headings large enough to be read from a distance of roughly 3 feet (1 meter)?

❏ Is your display typed?

❏ Is your display colorful, but not so flashy that it is distracting?

❏ Is your display neat?

❏ Is everything spelled properly?

Say It!

Name: _____ **Date:** _____

An exciting part of any science fair is the interview. During this question-and-answer session, a judge will ask you all about your project. It is important to practice your interviewing skills so that you can impress the judges!

Break up into pairs. With your partner, take turns acting out the roles of judge and the person being interviewed. Use the questions below as your guide.

Judge's Questions:

1. What is your project about?

_____

2. Why did you choose this project?

_____

3. How did you come up with the idea for your project?

_____

4. What was the purpose of your experiment?

_____

5. Did your experiment answer the main questions that you had before you began your project?

_____

6. What was your experiment procedure?

_____

7. How did you gather your data?

_____

8. Can you explain the data that you gathered?

_____

9. What conclusions have you drawn from your project?

_____

10. What new questions arose from your project? How could you extend your project to answer them?

_____

Science Fair Dos and Don'ts

Name: _____ **Date:** _____

The big day is almost here! People from outside of your school may be visiting your science fair. You will want to represent your school well. Make sure you know how to behave during the science fair.

☐ Do dress neatly.

☐ Do wait quietly until it is your turn to have your project judged.

☐ Do try to answer the judge's questions as best as you can.

☐ Don't talk or laugh loudly while you are waiting for the judges to come to your table.

☐ Don't play around with your display, or you might damage something before the judges even get to you.

☐ Don't chew gum.

☐ Don't be nervous. Just do your best.

☐ Do have fun!

Checklist: What to Bring on the Day of the Science Fair

Name: _____ **Date:** _____

Most displays need some setting up on the day of the fair. Gather the materials below to bring with you on science-fair day. Mark an "X" beside each item once you have packed it. If you don't need an item, cross it off your list.

❑ Your backboard

❑ Your project report

❑ Any models or other equipment that you want to include in your display

❑ Glue

❑ Stapler

❑ Heavy-duty tape

❑ Scissors

❑ Thumb tacks

❑ Pen

❑ Pencil

❑ A book to keep you occupied while you wait for the judges to visit you

❑ Extra markers

❑ Extra copies of your project summary

❑ Tools or electrical equipment to assemble your display (if needed)

❑ Electrical extension cord (if needed)

❑ Extra batteries (if needed)

Chapter 6

The Big Day and Beyond

Overview

Congratulations—you made it to the big day! The final chapter in this book will carry you over the finish line . . . and slightly beyond. In it you will find a judging rubric. It will give the experts who are evaluating student projects specific criteria upon which to base their judgments. This ensures that each project will be evaluated fairly and by the same standards. It also gives you solid reasoning for the judges' final decisions. That way, if a student questions his or her standing in the fair later, you can refer back to the rubrics to explain his or her project's strengths and weaknesses.

And, of course, once the judging is complete, you get to award the first-, second-, and third-place winners with their awards. How you choose to do so—whether in a formal ceremony in the school auditorium or in a more informal setting such as the classroom—is up to you. And finally, this chapter includes thank-you notes to send to your parent volunteers and judges for helping you pull off such a successful event.

How to Use This Chapter

Prior to the fair, decide upon how you will handle the judging process. If you have only one judge, he or she will judge every project. In that case, photocopy one rubric for each science-fair project. However, if you have more than one judge attending the fair, you might want to consider splitting up the judges so that each one judges an equal portion of the projects, or you could send judges around in teams.

If you plan to hand out awards to winners, make photocopies of the winner's award certificate provided in this chapter and then fill in the blanks with the winner's name, place, the date the award is given, and your signature. Consider printing the completed awards on high-quality paper and even framing them.

For participants who did not place—or if you did not judge the fair for first-, second-, and third-place winners—the participant's award certificate makes a nice keepsake for students and reminds them of their great achievement! Hand these awards out to all students who participated, regardless of how well their project turned out.

Lastly, photocopy the thank-you notes for parent volunteers and judges. Fill them in and send them out as soon as time permits.

Helpful Tip

Once the science fair is over, how can you tap into your students' creativity for your own benefit? Have every student turn his or her written report into a book for your classroom library. This will provide future students with a collection to browse for ideas and guidance. The collection will also give students a nice selection of reading material throughout the year if they finish written assignments early. Ask students to photocopy their written reports and place them inside a clear-covered binder. Have students make a colorful cover page for their books.

Judging Rubric

Name of Project: _____

Grade: _____

Student Name(s): _____

_____

Teacher: _____

1. Shares understanding of the scientific method through oral presentation

points	
4	Discusses the six main parts of the scientific method: hypothesis, variables, materials, procedure, data, and conclusions.
3	Discusses four or five parts of the scientific method.
2	Discusses two or three parts of the scientific method.
1	Does not seem to understand the scientific method.

2. Shows use of the scientific method through the backboard

points	
4	Clearly and neatly labels and displays the scientific method on the backboard.
3	Displays the scientific method on the backboard.
2	Has some steps to the scientific method on the backboard.
1	Lacks steps to the scientific method on the backboard.

3. Speaks knowledgeably about the project

points	
4	Shares many details of the project with the judge.
3	Shows clear understanding of the project.
2	Knows what the project is, but gives little explanation.
1	Tries to answer questions from the judge.

4. Presents data using well-organized tables, graphs, and charts

points	
4	Tables, graphs, and charts accurately and neatly display data.
3	Tables, graphs, and charts accurately display data.
2	Some tables, graphs, and charts are included on the board.
1	Lacks tables, graphs, and charts.

5. Shows enthusiasm and interest in the project

points	
4	Shows genuine enthusiasm for and interest in the topic. Offers suggestions for further investigation.
3	Shows genuine enthusiasm for and interest in the topic.
2	Seems interested in the project.
1	Does not seem to care about the project.

Points: _____ /20

Comments: _____

_____

_____

SCIENCE AWARD
Winner

This is to certify that

_____

has earned _____ place in

our school's science fair.

Congratulations

on a job well done!

Awarded on _____

Signed _____

Science Teacher

Science
Excellence

SCIENCE AWARD
Participant

This is to certify that

_____

has participated in

our school's science fair.

Congratulations

on a job well done!

Awarded on _____

Signed _____

Science Teacher

Science Excellence

From your child's science teacher

Thank You Letter

Dear Parent:

As you know, our science fair was a huge success—and I have you to thank! Pulling off a science fair is a large task. But with your help, we did it!

I appreciate that you volunteered to take part in such an important event.

Thanks again,

_____
(Science Teacher)

From the science teacher

Thank You Letter

Dear Judge:

As you know, our science fair was a huge success—and I have you to thank! Pulling off a science fair is a large task. But with your help, we did it!

I know that judging science-fair projects can be a challenge, especially when the children have worked so hard on their projects and all are eager to win. But you did a fantastic job of selecting the best of the best.

Thanks again,

_____
(Science Teacher)

Resources

Books

National Science Teachers Association. 2003. *Science Fairs Plus*. Arlington, Virginia: NSTA Press. ISBN: 0-87355-219-9. Grades K–8.

This book is for the teacher who is still debating the merits of a science fair. It pulls articles from various NSTA publications such as *Science Scope* that address questions such as: "What Have Researchers Been Saying About Science Fairs?" and others that offer alternatives to the traditional science fair.

Phillips, Greg, and Lorraine Hoffman. 2006. *Science Fair Projects*, Volume 1. Grand Rapids, Michigan: Milestone, an Imprint of Frank Schaffer Publications. ISBN: 0-7682-3206-6. Grades 6–8.

Looking for a classroom resource for your students to browse? If so, this book offers complete projects and details on how to perform each one, including tables and charts.

O'Leary, Nancy K., and Susan Shelly. 2003. *The Complete Idiot's Guide to Science Fair Projects*. New York, New York: Alpha Books. ISBN: 1-59257-137-9. Grades elementary through high school.

This guide covers all science disciplines and includes 50 experiments for all ages. Includes tips from choosing a project that's right for the individual to understanding what the judges are looking for.

Bochinski, Julianne Blair. 2005. *The Complete Workbook for Science Fair Projects*. Hoboken, New Jersey: John Wiley & Sons, Inc. ISBN: 0-471-27336-8. Grades 5–12.

With this guide, you'll get expert advice on choosing and researching a topic, finding a mentor, and performing an experiment.

VanCleave, Janice. 2003. *Janice VanCleave's A+ Science Fair Workbook and Project Journal*. Hoboken, New Jersey: John Wiley & Sons, Inc. ISBN: 0-471-46719-7. Grades 7–12.

This book extends beyond the grade range of most of the other recommended titles in this resource list. But it is included because it offers project ideas that may be suitable for advanced elementary or junior high students who are looking for challenging experiment ideas, such as studying aquatic respiration.

Web Sites

Find out how the National Science Teachers Association (NSTA) views science fairs by reading its official position statement:
http://www.nsta.org/positionstatement&psid=3

This simple, yet surprisingly helpful site offers interactive pages that help students find a topic area, narrow down topics, set up an experiment, and more. The site also provides mentoring tips for the most dedicated students and offers links to teacher resources.
http://www.sciencebuddies.org

This site from Discovery Education offers comprehensive tips for teachers, parents, and students as they prepare to host a science fair or complete a science-fair project.
http://school.discovery.com/sciencefaircentral

This online article, "Spark Science Fair Success," by Toby Leah Bochan walks parents through the ins and outs of science fairs.
http://content.scholastic.com/browse/article.jsp?id=1401

Answer Key

What Makes a Good Question? (p. 30)

Answers will vary.

How Did You Do That? (p. 32)

Answers will vary.

Perfecting Your Procedure (p. 33)

Answers will vary.

Stay Cool (p. 34)

1. 3
2. Type of container
3. Melting time
4. Plastic
5. Styrofoam cups keep ice cream from melting longest.

A-maze-ing Fish (p. 35)

1. Number of twists and turns
2. Time it takes for the fish to swim through the maze
3. One
4. Approximately 30 seconds
5. It takes a fish more time to swim through a maze that has many twists and turns compared with a maze that has fewer twists and turns.

Kitten Craze (p. 36)

1. Your kitten's age
2. Your kitten's weight
3. The amount of food and water given to the cat
4. Between the first and second weeks
5. Kittens gain more weight when they are younger than they do as they get older.

Sports Score (p. 37)

1. Badminton
2. 15
3. 5
4. Badminton, because fewer students prefer it over other sports
5. Students enjoy soccer most. Badminton is the least favorite among students.

Chocolate Lover's Experiment (p. 38)

Answers will vary.